SLIDE

SLIDE

Mark Pajak

CAPE POETRY

3 5 7 9 10 8 6 4 2

Jonathan Cape, an imprint of Vintage, is part of the Penguin Random House group of companies whose addresses can be found at global.penguinrandomhouse.com

Copyright © Mark Pajak 2022

Mark Pajak has asserted his right to be identified as the author of this Work in accordance with the Copyright, Designs and Patents Act 1988

First published by Jonathan Cape in 2022

penguin.co.uk/vintage

A CIP catalogue record for this book is available from the British Library

ISBN 9781787330313

Typeset in 11/13pt Bembo by Jouve (UK), Milton Keynes

Printed and bound in Great Britain by TJ Books Ltd, Padstow, Cornwall

The authorised representative in the EEA is Penguin Random House Ireland, Morrison Chambers, 32 Nassau Street, Dublin DO2 YH68

for Ian and Christie

the animals had eyes
and in their glance was permanence
John Berger

CONTENTS

I

RESET

She chafes a flame from the lighter,
listens to its gush of butane.

This thirteen-year-old,
hunkered down behind the P.E. hut.

For a full minute she watches
the raw egg-white heat quiver

round its yolk. Then she unthumbs
and the flame slims out.

She tugs back her sleeve on a scar,
a small pink socket in her forearm.

She holds her breath and plugs in
the hot lighter. Her lips clench white,

eyes into walnuts, the metal cap
fizzing into skin and fat and this

is how she deletes herself. Her mind's
blank page a kind of snow blindness.

Then, all her muscles go slack.
She opens her eyes for what feels

like the first time. Lets out the breath
taken in by someone else.

TRICK

Inside this disused tool-shed in Hammer Wood
slatted walls morse daylight on an earth floor.

Here two local boys find a knife, its blade
freckled in rust. The older boy picks it up,

with its egg whiff of wet metal, and points
to his friend to back against the wall *for a trick.*

Then the younger boy's T-shirt is hustled
over his head and rolled into a blindfold.

In its blackness, he imagines the moment held
like a knife above his friend's head. His friend

who whispers. *Don't. Move.* And then
there's a kiss. Lips quickly snipping against his.

Silence. He's aware of his chest, the negative
of his T-shirt. He pulls his blindfold. Looks

the older boy full in his up-close face. And sees
that he's bleeding, everywhere, under his skin.

CRYSTAL

Last orders. I put my cloth to a misty wineglass
and twist the shine in like a lightbulb.

At the end of my bar, a girl. Maybe twenty.
Her back turned on her pint, and a man's hand

spilling a powder. A hiss from an envelope
like a slow fuse. Her lager's fine chains of fizz

suddenly shake until all the liquid is the white tail
of a rattlesnake. But it's late. So I hold up

the wineglass. Fill it with the bar's dirty light.
Hang it on the rack where it slides to snap

against the bowl of another. That chime;
the sound of glass almost breaking. I slowly

twist and hang, twist and hang, with such
crystal concentration I nearly don't notice

when she finally stands to leave. Her spine wags
and is steadied by a man's hand. The last wineglass

is hung. Upside down, they are a line of bells
without tongues. Clear now. When she turns,

her face on his shoulder, she is younger than
eighteen. They leave behind her pint glass.

A last dreg. A spray of white. Asking to be
washed and polished and held up to the light.

A COTTON HANGING

Textile Gallery, Science and Industry Museum, Manchester

If you twist
twist

this 1861
curtain,

of Manchester
mills

and American
cotton,

into a tall
white

rope – then
let

go, it turns
turns

into a girl
dancing

in her long
dress

of Osnaburg
cloth;

her feet so
quiet

she could be
treading

on nothing
but

the hot
Alabama air.

EMBERS

Coniston, March 2020

The log in the fire
is like a grey bellied fish,
its gills breathing red.

AFTER CLOSING TIME

We head to the edge of town,
to the black river and old stone bridge.

Two boys full of vodka,
tipping side to side like flames.

And for a laugh, we climb
the railing and hang from our arms.

Below in the deep, two boys
peer up at us over their feet.

Like drops of water
we are gathering ourselves to fall.

One of us says, *You go first,*
and we echo this back and forth.

We are here for a very long time.
Years in fact. I marry. Divorce.

You skip all that, become a father.
We see less and less of each other.

Now we are what the world
considers 'men'. Which is to say

we've learnt that falling is inevitable.
Yet here we are still, side by side,

two boys way past closing time,
holding on until the other lets go.

THIN

Collie dog
locked
in a shed
in Toxteth.
Dead.
We shoved
the door in,
found him:
thin,
a bin-bag
of cutlery,
a cider-pint
stink. Flies
in the spoons
of his eye sockets.
Scraps of fur
crumbed
with blood.
Empty shelves
of ribs
and the pear-stalk
of his penis.
Dead. Until
I touched him
and he whined
like a knife
scraping a plate.
Rattled the rinds
of his tail.

II

CAT ON THE TRACKS

He wore the night in his fur, sat on a rung
between the rails, tail wisping like smoke

as a distant train split the air along its seam.
Its coming headlight laid down track

and placed an opal into each black seed
of the cat's eyes, every blink slow as an eclipse.

Soon the white light pinned him, the only drop
of night left as vibration turned the rails to mercury.

But there was no give in the cat, no flex anywhere
but his tail. And for a moment their roles reversed,

as though it were the train facing the inevitable cat,
the end of the line. The world lit up like a page

and the train a sentence before the full-stop.

SPITTING DISTANCE

Near Edale, I find a live rifle shell
like a gold seed in the earth.

So I load it into my mouth
and go on walking, the sun

breathing down my neck,
the head of Mam Tor rising

and the path falling like a braid.
So this is what it's like to be a gun:

copper bleeding on the gums,
the domino click in the teeth.

At the blue summit, I look down
with my new perspective

on the warped floor of Derbyshire,
to where a village pools in a valley

and a chimney hangs from the sky
on a white string. And I watch

with hunger the red dot of a car
stop at a crossroads. I suck hard

on the blunt bud, drawing out
its deeper flavour of powder,

smoke down the barrel
of my throat. Then it hits me

that there's another side to this.
And I lie in the warm heather.

A body with a bullet
in its head staring at this sky.

Its clouds blown open.
Its sudden night.

POEM

A decade of moorland crosswind
and the slow iron bar bend of a tree.

More than patience, this is craft; branches
blown like glass into brittle intricacies.

NETTLE FUZZ

I fell into a nettle-pit,
face-down in serrated leaves and black stems.

Up-close I could see the nettle hairs,
a white fuzz round their edges like a constant hum.

But the only sound was the slow laugh of a crow
and wind like applause through the ash trees.

You can only hear a nettle through the skin;
each hair triggers a finger like a tuning fork

and I stood up with tinnitus shivering in every muscle.

INTO THE MUDFLATS

The *East Anglian Daily Times* gave no name,
just: 'photography student, twenty', and that she
had walked from Ipswich. Followed the Orwell
here, where its mouth breathes out sea.

Maybe she could have showed you in her camera
how the last mile of riverbank lost distinction.
Became this grey area between land and water:
islands of pale grass and a salty sewer reek

which even on days without wind reaches far inland.
Beautiful. Maybe that's what she thought.
And perhaps she was trying to bound island to island
towards the snapshot of a cormorant on a rock.

All that's certain is, she left the path. Then a slip
or a missed foot, and her leg would have dipped
easy as a spoon in soup. She could have pulled
at the grass and unlaced white roots. Screamed

heat up her throat, as cold swallowed her knees.
But it would have been evening then and the sun
sinking too. And there'd have been a moment,
at that low angle of daylight, when the mudflats lit up

like quicksilver. So bright, she might have stopped
screaming. It really would have been beautiful then.
And if someone, anyone, had come running,
they might have seen her paused, waist-deep;

her torso blacked out, flat and simple like a stencil
on the wet shine. Like the half-sunk silhouettes
on all those signs. All those luminous warning signs
put up after the search.

FENCE

I am the city boy on a school trip amazed
by this distance: Cheshire tiled green
with farmland and a blue sky that opens
in my chest. I've wandered off, curious
of this field, its strange crop of white hummocks
– a herd of sun-drunk cows. I hear the fence
sizzle before I see it. Then it's there,
its posts like frets of a guitar. Each sign's

DO NOT TOUCH enough to make me want to.
I hover my hand. Feel a change in weather.
Years from now I'll try to think of my first
kiss – and my mind will blow a fuse, recall
this finger-tip, this warm lip of metal
and the stone-smooth moment of my stopped heart.

DRIFT

Saddleworth, February 2018

Outside, the evening snows and the hillside
fills like a sail; the level ground rises
with the depth, the moor slowly unmoored.

MOUNTAIN PATH

We've all passed
on this path.
This sometimes
sheep-path. This
other times red-
deer path. This
almost nothing,
trickle of a path.

This less grass
than there, path.
This wet drag
of tangled ferns
across the chest
path. This, losing
its thread like
a grandmother's story

path. This, in then
out of furry
nettles, path.
This lemon whiff
of bruised leaf
path. This walked
into existence
by those who came

before, path. This
pressure of each
boot remembered
in smooth earth
path. This decade
after decade
becoming clearer
but still after centuries

not clear enough
path. This suddenly
lost – shin-deep
in itchy capillary
branches of heather
– path. This cannot
be followed, only
learned, path. This
path that we all
pass on.

III

THE TILT

Those days when Mum's hangover
was a dark kitchen, sat at the table,
head in her hands like a full bowl,

I'd slip out of the house and come here:
this bookshop on Luke Street.
In here I could shut the world

with a door and be walled in by hardbacks,
their spines full of broken capillaries.
Paperbacks neat as piano keys.

In here it was quiet. Floorboards
tense as a frozen lake. The book
in my chest that opened and closed.

And I'd kneel to a low shelf,
choose at random and break open
a loaf of paper. It didn't matter

that I couldn't afford it, or that soon
the owner would make me leave,
or that I was only four and couldn't read.

The smell of an old book is a memory of trees.
A boy can tilt into it, the way a drunk
tilts her glass, and lean back emptied.

A SET PLACE

Tonight, to show her husband she is expecting,
     my aunt is setting
an extra place at their dinner table.

On the cooker, blue flames tickle under a pot
the lid just starting to stutter
     sweet smell of carrots going soft.

And because ultimately
     the pregnancy will fail
allow her this set place to put things on hold:

here, let the clean knife
     hold a sliver of ceiling in its blade;
let all the dining room

be trapped in the bubble
     of the wineglass;
and let the fork hold open its little silver palm;

as this wooden chair
with the plush bump of a cushion in its lap
     holds no one.

THE LEMON GAME

Here is a sweet apple, sweet-thing,
says the boy's mother, once again.
But as always, she drops down a lemon
green and yellow like an old bruise.

And the boy must palm it up in a bite;
wax-skin bursting, wetting him chin
to small chest, his mouth mulling
the stinging taste, its soggy chomp

nothing like an apple's crunch;
but she studies his face, referees
his face, pores over his face, and he
knows the rules.

It must not screw up like a fist.
It must not screw up like a fist.

CAMPING ON ARRAN, 1992

Dad, you had shared with me your sleeping bag.
And we lay like hands held in one pocket.
When the dark flickered and a moment's pause

before thunder: like the sky waking.
And waking with it, I trembled; trapped,
a boy in a storm, in this tight space

ripe with your sleeping man's body.
But when the canvas flared again
white with a hem of shadow grass,

you were awake and counting
down the seconds to thunder.
And I, listening, was struck still.

As each count became less
– the storm brighter, louder –
I could feel a closeness

like breath in the air.
And I fell asleep
as rain would fall; soft,

then in a rush.
You counting us
into the eye.

VEGETATION

There is a Peace Lily on my desk.
This morning, each green blade
is velveted with dust. As a grandson,
I know how The Still can attract dust.
I know how to smooth a washcloth
over skin, so easily torn.
I know that morning after morning
there may seem to be no movement

but sometimes the afternoon will fall
through the curtains in a slope of sunlight,
so strong it lights up every drifting
spore and fibre, and I will walk in
to find that this senseless thing
has leant a little closer to the window.

THE STILL

1. *Still Life*

In the fruit
on Gran's bedside table,
under the translucent skin
of a grape,
the black pips
at the core
seem to be crawling.

What's going on
inside the greenlit gum
of its flesh
are six ants:
the whiskers
of their legs,
their small
plectrum heads
and snipping mouths.

Soon all the fruit bowl
will be moving.
Already
an apple's breast
has a visible pulse.
A once-dense peach
is deflating.

And what can she do
but stare
from her hospital bed;
seeming all the stiller
for her slow
pink eyelids,
those quick
teaspoon
breaths.

2. *Night Bus*

At a red light, I don't notice the finger-drum of engine pistons
until they stop. And for this stalled moment the bus

becomes a church; that stillness of twenty seated strangers
holding silence in the same direction. Then traffic lights

drop into green, ignition ripples in the black windows
and the wheels begin their cassette crackle of bad road.

Still, at the next hard stop in the service, every head
dips in unison. We all witness the same old woman shuffle on.

Her cane like the timid leg of a deer. Each step, a white
wince of teeth. Then, one by one, coins spin themselves flat

in the driver's plate. Her face bows to his stall. Lips
nibble soft words. Asking, please, to be taken from this place.

3. *My Dead Grandmother*

Here is a rope-swing; its blue plait slung
from a branch. Sat there on its knot,
bare feet planted on the riverbank, is Gran.

Stood beside her, my dad watches the river
– its spate frayed white on small rocks –
his eyes black pebbles under thick glasses.

But Gran's eyes are full of distance, watching
nothing. Her gown breathes-in the breeze,
and her hospice reek, that chemical rot,

meets my father's face thick as damp cloth.
But he says nothing. Just lets the river whisper
its shush of water. Then he gives his *wee mammy*

a push. The swing halves the air like paper.
And as she moves away, her weight
just enough to crack the rope's long spine,

my dad, left behind on the riverbank,
is both the man watching the swing go
and the boy aching for the swing back.

DELICACY

That long squeal from the lobster
under the pot's fluttery lid, is just
steam singing through the slats
in its armour. There is no actual

feeling there. It is the same principle
as the resonance chamber
in a factory whistle. Like the one
that used to scream a pillar of mist

above the old Leyland's car plant
and only then would my grandfather realise
he'd been cutting metal for twelve hours:
staring down at his red gauntlets,

the PVC shine on their outer-shells,
and with a shock he'd remember
the hands, the naked hands inside;
the clammy, white and delicate flesh.

IV

A COUNTRY LANE

Its single track, privet hedges, broken tarmac and a distant hiss
is suddenly a red car — already gone and the sun-flash
of its outline fading in the black of each blink. Its rush,
far-off again, lapses like a sigh. The hedges slowly nod to a stop.

Then, just like that, I step into the lane and lay down; my back
to the rough road's store of heat. And I stare through the closed pink
of my lids. Breathe; and hear all the slits in my teeth.
So I hold my breath and try to listen down the road. There is

no wind. The fields are full of silent wheat. I'm listening so hard
it's as if I am trying to hear the future. But all I can hear
is the nothing that's coming. Louder and louder. And the longer I wait
the more my held-breath aches; like a foot on my heart

as it accelerates.

DARE

You dare me to cross Bentley Road naked.
It's three a.m. and we're the only two awake
under streetlights with cough-drop orange bulbs.

It's icy. The frozen road shines like treacle
and my penis has slunk like a hand into its sleeve.
Each bare foot lifts with a slight adhesive rip.

But when I reach you waiting on the opposite kerb
with your arms full of my clothes, your bashful head
bowed but your side-on eye unblinking as a fish,

the streetlight's glow has a whisky warmth.
Your brow sweats. My wet mouth steams open.
And I dare you. I dare you.

THRESHOLD

Last night, I don't remember
being woken by the brakes
or the tyres squealing away.

But in the quiet aftermath
I did hear the small voice of a cat.
And though she called out

to the street in a language
just as strange and half-formed
as a baby's, one still bruised and sore

from the trauma of its birth,
I knew exactly what
she was pleading and pleading for.

THE KNACK

Between the cattle shed
and the freezer room
there is a small concrete yard
where a man
lifts his sledgehammer
and rests its head
gently against a cow's left temple
just behind her dark eye
and there is a knack to this

like how a waiter
pulls off that tablecloth trick
it's all in the planted feet and the wrists
then just one
deft swipe
and the cloth is gone
before the plates and glasses
can catch on
and this takes practice

this takes accidents
and the occasional long bottle
rolling on its side
as its head
spills a thick black pulse of wine
but maybe
this is all a bad example
because a bottle's
slender throat and shoulders

are a little too human
because this
is just a cow
just the large eye of a cow
where each slow blink coats the lens with light
her lens full of staring dark
and because this hammer
is never deft
never taking just one swipe.

A PILE OF LEAVES

Suddenly in the headlights a pile of leaves
takes on the semblance of a sleeping tramp
and I am through him before I can stop.
Then in the rear-view mirror that horror-show red
of brake-lights against the hedges
as exploded leaves flit and swirl like a flock of bats.

Later, as I go on driving home, I think
if a settled pile of leaves can take on that semblance
then the opposite must also be true:
as in Princes Park last winter, where the children
dragged sledges through the derelict trees
and, for two days, passed a still heap under the first snow.

TICKLING THE CANAL

Lured to the canal on her dad's yarn
of Alaska and how he'd tickled fish

from icy rivers. And though this is only Bootle,
Liverpool, and rats wicker in the reeds,

a mallard rasps and a condom
eels by on the current, she thinks herself Inuit

in this northern wind that shivers the water
as a magnet will skitter iron shavings.

So she dips her small hands, motions
as if beckoning and waits for the trout.

But there are no trout. Instead, in the sunk
smoke of algae, sticklebacks scatter

like a shoal of razors. Under the drowned
hull of a bathtub, a pike as long as her arm

slys its snout upwards. The rusty ring
of its gullet ready to slip on a finger.

AS MY FRIEND DRIVES THE HOT MILE OF CASTLE STREET AND NOTHING IS SAID

I listen to the skim of his palm on the leather steering wheel.
How the indicator *tuts* as the car leans into a new lane.
At a red light the engine blurs through my seat, and my friend

sucks a cigarette-ember one breath closer; the faint static crackle
of tobacco fibres. He watches a woman cross over. Then between drags
he says *I don't mind blacks, it's her breed I can't stomach.*

The lights change. The brakes open and the stillness in our car gives an inch
before we accelerate. Under our tyres, the soft rolling grain of road.
Through his grip, the occasional spinning hiss of the wheel

as my friend drives the hot mile of Castle Street and nothing is said.

SILVER

Her black Audi under an amber streetlamp;
its engine ticks like ice in whisky.
And now that she has gone inside her townhouse,
he crosses the street.
A key pinched in his finger and thumb;
the thumbnail squeezing itself pale.

The driver's door is smooth and slippery with light;
so he applies the key-tip
until the metal concedes a slow dimple.
All he has to do is walk the car's flank
to drag a thin rasp through the paintwork.
He thinks he will feel better.

But all he feels in his pinch, in the vibration,
is a hotel room two years ago.
The single malt she'd been drinking
all the night before, still sticky on his lips.
And she asks him to zip the back on her dark dress.
Just this simple, intimate act

sealed up in the buzz of his thumb,
as it trails a line of silver through the black.

V

THE SCREAM

Like so many of us it has kettled in her chest
all her life. She takes it to the River Ouse.

Through the shallows her footsteps smoke
in the silt. The pockets of her overcoat fat

with the rattle of small stones. She walks
her head under. In the green dust of deeper water

riverweed ribbons downstream. A shoal
of minnows circles slow as a mirror-ball.

She stands in the loose orbit of her long skirt.
Head fluent with hair. When finally she lets it

out: a glow through her throat. But the sound
dulls in water and she only overhears her

distant self. And then the scream is in little
flickery pieces above her. Like drops of solder

these rising bubbles melt together. On the surface,
flat water blisters into four floating globes.

Before, one by one, the scream delicately stops.

BROOD

At sixteen, I did a day's work
on an egg farm.
A tin shed the size of a hangar.

Inside its oven dark
two thousand stacked cages,
engines of clatter and squawk.

My job, to shine a torch
through the bars for the dead hens
then pack them tight into a bin-bag.

All the time my mind chanting:
there's only one hen, just one
ruined hen repeated over and over.

In this way I soothed the sight
of all that caged battery,
their feathers stripped to stems,

their patches of scrotum skin,
their bodies held
in the dead hands of their wings.

But what kept me awake
that hot night in my box room,
as I listened to the brook outside

chew on its stones and the fox's
human scream, was how
those thousand-thousand birds

had watched me. And really
it was me repeated over and over,
set in the amber of their eyes.

Me, the frightened boy in jeans
stiff with chicken shit, carrying
a bin-bag full of small movement.

A foot that opened. An eyelid
that unshelled its blind nut.
A beak mouthing a word.

SLAUGHTER-HOUSE WORKER
AT THE PUBLIC POOL

The showers
stopped him dead.
It wasn't
what you'd think:
the sterile white
of the tiled walls,
that neat line
of pink bodies,
a gleam
of metal
over each one.

It was the smell.
How the sweetness
of chlorine and disinfectant
comes so close
to wiping out
that other smell: faint
but warm
and unmistakably
animal.
It was that,
that and the constant
guttering
of the drains.

OPEN WATER

The underside of a rowboat
is the shape of a church door
to the world below;

how many have opened
for a man to fall out of a storm
into that deep quiet.

WRECK

Tonight, anger
is dark water
full of silent
pull in the tilted
forests of kelp,
and down
here, past
jellyfish
white as
Chinese lanterns
and the bottomless
plummet
of coastal shelf,

I am staring up
at the top
floor light
of her
bedroom window.

★

The delicate
silver spine
down her
favourite
black dress,
how easily
her other man
splits it:

the way
dark water
falls open
in the wake
of a boat.

MINIMUM WAGE

Chef has gone.
Again
I am handless
in the dishwater,

the weightless
clack of plates.
Soap suds
frittering into nothing.

And just these
two blue bars
in the Fly-killer.
One day

I mean to leave.
To sit
on a riverbank
where the shallows are so clean

a carp
hovers over his own shadow.
And the water
only becomes visible

behind the slow shake
of his tail,
where the surface breaks into an eddy
and spins.

Some things are so fast
they seem still,
this little whirlpool
like the stem of a wineglass.

Until the swirl
becomes
a plughole
and the sink has drained.

Again
that whiff like singed hair
as the blue light winces
on a sizzling moth.

I am stacking plates,
thinking
how neatly
one emptiness
fits into the next.

NOTES & ACKNOWLEDGEMENTS

The book's epigraph is from John Berger's 'They Are the Last'.

'Reset' was commended in the 2019 National Poetry Competition. 'Trick' was commended in the 2020 National Poetry Competition. 'A Cotton Hanging' was written in response to two exhibitions, one from the Science and Industry Museum in Manchester and one from the International Slavery Musuem in Liverpool. 'Cat on the Tracks' was commended in the 2014 National Poetry Competition. 'Spitting Distance' won first place in the 2016 Bridport Prize. 'Mountain Path' was part of a sequence commissioned by Windfall Films for the 'The Great Mountain Sheep Gather', which aired in April 2020 on the BBC. 'The Lemon Game' was commended in the 2014 Buzzwords Cheltenham Poetry Competition. 'Camping on Arran, 1992' is for my father. 'Vegetation' and 'The Still' are for Mary. 'Dare' was commended in the 2017 Poetry London Competition. 'Tickling the Canal' is for my mother – who did almost lose a finger when she was a child. 'After Closing Time' is for Joe.

Thanks to New Writing North whose award of a substantial Northern Writers' Award helped with the writing of the first half of this book. Thanks to the Society of Authors whose award of another grant helped with the writing of the second half. Also, thanks to the Kraków UNESCO City of Literature Residency Program 2018, where some of these poems began.

Thanks to Robin Robertson for all his guidance, belief and patience.

Thanks, so much, to Michael Symmons Roberts, and to The Peggy Poole Award for a year's worth (and then some) of invaluable mentorship.

Thanks also to Iris Skipworth, Natalie Burdette, Ian Humphries, Scott Fellows, Keith Hutson, Andrew McMillan, Helen Mort, Kim Moore, Lee Thompson, Jess Green, Cooper and all the others who provided help and advice with writing over the years.

Thanks to the editors of the following publications and anthologies in which earlier versions and reprints of some of these poems appeared: *Buzz Words – Poems about Insects* (Everyman's Library Pocket Poets), *Guardian, Kontent, London Review of Books, The North, Off the Shelf – A Celebration of Bookshops in Verse, Rialto, The 'C' Word, The Long White Thread of Words – Poems for John Berger.*

Thanks to Carol Ann Duffy and Ruth Hartnoll for making me believe I could do this.